The Little Gita of Problem Solving

The Little Gita of Problem Solving

By Sirshree Tejparkhi

Copyright © Tejgyan Global Foundation
All Rights Reserved 2017

Tejgyan Global Foundation is a charitable organization
with its headquarters in Pune, India.

Published by WOW Publishings Pvt. Ltd., India

First edition published in May 2017

Second reprint in June 2018

Copyrights are reserved with Tejgyan Global Foundation and publishing rights are vested exclusively with WOW Publishings Pvt. Ltd. This book is sold subject to the condition that it shall not by way of trade or otherwise, be lent, resold, hired out, or otherwise circulated without the publisher's prior written consent in any form of binding or cover other than that in which it is published and without a similar condition including this condition being imposed on the subsequent purchaser and without limiting the rights under copyright reserved above, no part of this publication may be reproduced, stored in or introduced into a retrieval system, or transmitted, in any form, or by any means, electronic, mechanical, photocopying, recording or otherwise, without the prior written permission of both the copyright owner and the above-mentioned publisher of this book. Any person who does any unauthorized act in relation to this publication may be liable to criminal prosecution and civil claims for damages.

Contents

SECTION I
THE ROLE OF PROBLEMS IN LIFE

1. Introduction — 3
2. Purpose of Problems — 5
3. The Art of Viewing Problems — 9

SECTION II
18 SOLUTIONS TO ANY PROBLEM

4. The Little Gita of Problem Solving — 21
   - Solution 1: Increase Patience — 22
   - Solution 2: Gather Right Information — 25
   - Solution 3: Analyze the Root Cause — 27
   - Solution 4: Work Vigorously for a Few Days — 31
   - Solution 5: Persevere and Persist — 32
   - Solution 6: Revisit Your Goal — 34
   - Solution 7: Change Your Perspective — 36
   - Solution 8: Identify the Unexpected — 40

Solution 9: Sow the Seed of Faith	43
Solution 10: Reframe Your Self-talk	45
Solution 11: Convert Hurt to Humor	47
Solution 12: Identify the Obstacle Wall	50
Solution 13: Retain the Happy Hat and Be in Gratitude	54
Solution 14: Increase Your Backup Power	57
Solution 15: Prayer and Meditation	63
Solution 16: Awaken Faith and Devotion	67
Solution 17: Become a DS Master	71
Solution 18: Surrender	76
5. The Ultimate Remedy to Dissolve Your Problems	79

SECTION I

THE ROLE OF PROBLEMS IN LIFE

1

Introduction

While going through various situations in life, we all come across a variety of problems. Some have problems to do with their children, siblings or parents. Some have problems with their colleagues, subordinates or boss. Students have problems with their peers. Employees have problems with their jobs. Businessmen have problems running their businesses and outdoing competition. Housewives have their own problems dealing with their household chores.

Students have problems with performing in their exams to score good marks. Eligible bachelors have their own problems. While married people tackle their relationship issues, aged people have health related problems. Thus, problems differ from one age group to the other. Children's problems are different from those of adults.

Problems also differ from one profession to the other. Architects have different problems vis-à-vis teachers, bankers, doctors, IT professionals or government employees. Further, the problems of employees are different from those of their managers.

There are many who are gripped by mental stress, fear, and anxiety. Some have financial hurdles in meeting their needs on time. Some have problems in retaining their financial position. Some have problems in maintaining harmony in their relationships. There are some who are wandering in search of peace. They look for remedy to their problems in the form of meditations, listening to spiritual discourses, reading self-help or philosophical literature, chanting of mantras, singing hymns.

Looking at this plethora of problems, one may consider problems to be an integral part of life and life without problems seems next to impossible for them. As they believe, so do they experience. Their life is dominated by problems. As soon as they overcome one problem, another problem immediately creeps into their life. They keep seeking the silver lining of happiness on the horizon of a life rid with problems. They believe life to be a game of snakes and ladders. If they can overcome the snakes in their life, then alone can they be happy. But such a life is consumed by stress and they fall victim to anxiety and misery.

Let's understand it with an example of a student.

The student is always stressed to consistently perform better in his studies. If he fails to perform, then his career will be at stake. After he finishes his studies, he has to get a job. Then he is stressed to perform well at work.

Thus, we can see that everyone comes across a medley of problems in their life. Problems cause people to remember God and pray for resolution to their ongoing problem.

What if you discovered that there are higher and better ways of resolving problems, approaches that will enable you to not just solve your problems, but *dissolve* them? Unbelievable? This book gives you that magical wand of a new outlook which makes problems appear as challenges or opportunities in your life. You will learn the very purpose of problems and various strategies to arrive at solutions to resolve them.

2

Purpose of Problems

When we are overwhelmed with problems, we may feel that we are the only one who has problems, everyone else is better off, if not happy. But, that's not the case. Everyone has problems at some time or the other. If everyone has to go through problems, there must be some reason behind the very purpose problems occur in our life.

We have come to this world with a grand objective. We need to experientially know who we truly are and express divine qualities like love, joy, peace, abundance, courage, confidence, communication, creation, patience that lie latent within us. We need to completely open up and blossom in our life.

Some of the events or situations that you view negatively are actually the results of your higher thoughts for growth, for realizing your innate potential. For example, if you've strongly held the intention to succeed in your career in a short time, you very well may be confronted with a series of challenges for this to happen. However, when you do not connect these challenges with your deep intentions to grow, you would probably view these growing pains and the stress related to them negatively as problems.

In reality, problems appear because of your orders for growth. In this case, they are part of your orders for a rapidly successful career. There are skills, knowledge and experiences you must gain, before you can succeed in your career. Every setback, frustration, challenge, obstacle or struggle, becomes a powerful teacher and an elevating springboard. This understanding will help you entertain only happy thoughts even in the midst of struggle.

All the events that we encounter in our life are handcrafted to enable us to evolve and make progress and mature in life. However, due to our wrong beliefs and tendencies, we consider these events as problems. Sometimes, we are not mature enough to handle those events. The moment we look at them as a problem, we mentally shrink and withdraw. When we feel negatively, we introduce blocks in the onset of the solution. The solution to the problem gets obstructed when we feel disappointed. Thus, the situation deteriorates tenfold. We get bogged down by the problems and find ourselves tied down and helpless.

Sometimes, while traversing on the path of progress, we get stranded in between. We become reluctant to move forward. We lose sight of the objective of our journey amidst mundane and trivial matters. In this slumber, most of us start believing that we know everything and live in our own complacent world. Thus, instead of solving problems, we can get entangled in them.

At such times, life wakes us up from our slumber by imposing "problem" scenarios. As we change our outlook, we realize that problems have not come to let us down, they have come to move us forward in life. Because of problems, we are forced to take a pause to reflect and rethink on our life. If required, we enhance our physical strength, mental flexibility, sharpen our intellect, learn some new skills, gain some spiritual understanding in order to overcome those problems.

Sometimes, problems help us realize that the direction in which we were moving forward was not aligning with our goal and that we need to reorient our focus in the right direction. As we go on resolving every problem in our life, we find ourselves open up to a new door of opportunities. Then we thank the problems for allowing us to expose ourselves to these new avenues of life. We say, "It's good that it happened. Had I not encountered this problem, I wouldn't have progressed in my life." Instead of lamenting over the problems first and then commending them, it's better to change our outlook of viewing problems at the outset.

Let's understand this with an example.

A sculptor decides to carve out an idol out of a stone. He first finalizes his design. Then he gets hold of a suitable stone. Then in the "roughing out" stage of the sculpting process, he uses hammer and chisel to remove the unnecessary part of the stone. Once the general shape of the idol has been determined, the sculptor uses other tools to refine the figure.

In the "refining" stage, he uses a chisel to add texture to the figure. Eventually he changes the stone from a rough block into the general shape of the finished idol. In the "finishing" stage, he uses other tools to enhance the shape into its final form. He uses sweeping strokes to remove excess stone as small chips or dust. Then he finishes the carving process by polishing the idol. Thus, after relentless effort, a superior quality idol comes into shape.

What the sculptor does with the stone is what problems do with us in order to shape us into evolved and mature human beings. The Renaissance artist Michelangelo claimed that his job was to free the human form hidden inside the block. Similarly, problems come to break us out of our mechanical life and limited beliefs, to chisel out our limitations and shortcomings and polish our virtues in the process of going through life's trials.

Once we understand the purpose of problems in our life, our outlook of viewing problems will change. We will learn a new art of looking at problems. We will stop considering a problem to be a problem. We will look at it as a challenge or an opportunity to help us progress further. Thereafter, every incident will become instrumental for our progress. The same problem, which used to delude us earlier, will begin to appear as a stepping-stone to move further on our path of progress.

Till we reach the ultimate state of development, it can greatly help to consider all problems as a springboard on our path of progress. Thereafter, all the problems will begin to dissolve on their own. We will find that the problems in our life have spontaneously disappeared.

3

The Art of Viewing Problems

Once we understand the purpose of problems in our life, it is essential to learn the art of viewing problems so that we can change our outlook towards them. Sometimes, changing our perspective is enough to solve the problem. With a higher perspective, the same situation, which appeared to be painful earlier, could stop seeming painful. We could gain an insight to rip through the problem, which can then unravel the diamonds hidden within it. As we become more proficient in the art of viewing problems, we become richer with these diamonds. And of course, as a bonus, our problems will also get solved.

You might wonder what these diamonds are. If one keeps getting diamonds on every problem he solves, how rich will he become! Indeed, he will become rich, but not in monetary terms but in terms of wisdom and maturity. Let's understand what these diamonds are.

Every problem conceals five diamonds viz. a solution, a gift, a ladder, a lesson, and a challenge.

THE FIRST Diamond: A Solution

Every problem has a solution hidden within it. This means that the cure to a disease can be found in the disease itself, the answer to a question can be unearthed in the question itself. Let's understand this with the help of some examples.

Diamond is one of the hardest materials and there was a time when cutting it was a major problem. The solution was found in the diamond itself. A diamond saw made of diamond dust was (and still is) used to cut diamonds. Similarly, you may have heard that poison can be used to make the antidote for the poison itself. If a scorpion stings you, then the antidote to the sting is found within the scorpion itself. The antidote to a snakebite lies in the venom of the snake itself! Also, vaccines are made from the same organism that they are supposed to protect from.

Another example: when someone is unable to digest a particular fruit, the solution lies in the fruit itself. If you begin to feel uneasy or unwell after eating a watermelon, then chew five to six watermelon seeds right there and that will solve your problem. The problem emerged from the watermelon and so did the solution.

If you are unable to digest a fruit without its peel, say a guava, then it should be eaten along with its peel. Likewise, if a fruit causes problems with peel, then it should be eaten after peeling. If bananas cause a problem, then after eating a banana, remove some pulp from the inner side of the banana skin and eat it. This will prevent any trouble due to the banana.

Let us look at one more example.

A person was traveling in a car and its tyre got punctured. He stopped by the side, removed the four nuts of the tyre and kept them aside. By chance, these nuts fell into the drainage flowing along the edge of the road. Now he did not know what to do. A young boy passing by asked him, "What happened? Do you need help?" The man looked at the boy doubtfully as he appeared naïve. He did not feel that this boy could help him. Nevertheless, he explained his situation. The boy said, "No big deal! Just remove one nut from each of the remaining three tyres and use them to fasten the spare tyre. In this way, your car will safely reach a mechanic's workshop." The man was taken aback. The solution was so simple. It did not require a highly developed intellect, just some common sense. Thus, the problem came from the car and so did the solution.

These were some examples that demonstrate how the solution can be hidden within the problem. Quite often, common sense plays a major role in finding the solution. Many a time, great scientists fail to find a simple solution, whereas an ordinary person unknowingly ends up making a great discovery.

If you are faced with a failure or a setback, you might wonder how the solution can lie within the problem, how the answer can lie within the question? But this is a fact. It has been seen that many students do not read questions attentively and end up writing the wrong answers in their exams. Then they wonder why they scored poorly. In most cases, the solution emerges as soon as the problem is correctly understood.

Whenever a problem arrives, raise your awareness and look deeper to be able to grasp the solution hidden within the problem itself. In the beginning you may find it difficult to understand this and find a solution that may be very subtle. But as your faith rises, this fact will begin to manifest before you.

Those who are crime detectives know the fact that in order to catch the criminal they first need to get to the scene of crime. The criminal is sought at the place of the crime because that is where the clues are found and often the criminal too returns to the scene of the crime. These detectives very well know that the solution lies in the problem itself. Thus, they find solutions many a time at the scene of crime.

THE SECOND Diamond: A Gift

Every problem arrives with the purpose of giving us a gift. In ignorance, we don't identify the gift and lament over the problem. We feel miserable if we have failed an exam, failed to get a promotion, lost a job, and so forth. If we look back and analyze the events from our past, we will realize that the events that we considered as problems and unnecessarily fretted over, have actually given us gifts. Everything was happening beautifully and we were getting anxious for no reason.

Now, we need to attempt to identify that gift in every problem. You may have heard that plants that withstand many storms grow into strong trees. Those plants that never get to deal with any storm can be uprooted by the mildest of storms. Similarly, those who face no problems in their lives remain unchallenged, stunted and immature. Only those who have been weathered by problems learn and mature to move ahead in life. While working on the situation at hand, you will unravel the gift of qualities like perseverance, courage, consistency, commitment, confidence, dedication and a strong character. These virtues will help you make further progress.

Whenever a problem arrives, ask yourself, "What's the gift in it for me?" The gift is always there in the problem. You just need to develop the eye, the right perspective, of seeing the truth behind the problem. Once you go to the origin of the problem, you will witness an everlasting joy in the light of which it becomes easier to dissolve your problems.

THE THIRD Diamond: A Ladder

Every problem is like a ladder that leads you to the pinnacle of success. This can be compared to a springboard used to take a dive into the water. The diving board is placed depending on how big you intend to dive. The bigger the leap, the higher you place the springboard. The springboard is thus made according to the person who is going to take the dive.

Just like the springboard, you can use every problem as a medium to climb the ladder of success. The peak of Self Expression (expression of your true divine Self) is scaled only through problems. Hence consider every problem as an opportunity to express divine qualities that are lying dormant within you and thereby derive happiness.

Just like the bull, which keeps moving in circles anticipating that it's doing a lot of work, many people too are busy in their daily grind. They live an unconscious life and consider themselves to be all-knowing. They keep sleepwalking in circles and believe that they are making progress.

Problems arrive to awaken us from such slumber. We are forced to contemplate whether our life is aligned with our grand mission on earth or whether we have got stuck in worthless pursuits. We can then make every problem instrumental for our growth and scale the peak of Self-expression.

In order to cross a marshy patch, you drop a stone in it and use it as a stepping stone to cross the patch and move ahead. Similarly, the problem too is a stepping stone; you can step on it and get out of the marshy patch of your life.

Until we achieve complete development, we should not consider things that trouble us as problems, but rather as stepping-stones or a springboard. By stepping on it we can take a leap to reach the peak of progress. Whenever you feel stressed, don't consider it as a problem. Instead, understand that it is a ladder that can raise you higher; it has come to get some work done through you; it has come to unravel the hidden qualities within you.

Once you have understood the true significance of problems arriving in your life, then later whenever you are faced with a problem, you will be thanking it. You will say, "It's good that this happened! If that problem had not cropped up, I would never have moved ahead. I was about to stop praying, thinking, contemplating, listening to the Truth, walking the path of Truth and helping others." Hence, you should always be alert that whenever something troubles you, then without being troubled by it, you should make it a ladder.

The world is a game of snakes and ladders, and spirituality is the knowledge to convert snakes into ladders. The snakes in our life are failures, problems, or setbacks that prevent us from attaining true happiness. These snakes can be converted into ladders to attain happiness and success.

THE FOURTH Diamond: A Lesson

A problem is not a troublemaker, but a teacher. In every failure there lies a hidden lesson. Whenever a problem arrives, ask yourself, "What's the lesson for me in this situation?"

If someone has a financial problem and he questions himself, "What is the lesson for me in this problem?" He then learns financial planning and proper investment. He also develops respect for money, the habit of saving, and the habit of not spending on worthless pursuits. Now, these habits can forever free him from his financial problems.

If someone has a health problem, he can learn from his illness too. If such a person learns the importance of regular exercises, then he will enjoy good health for the rest of his life.

Someone fails at work due to his inability to complete his project work on time. From this failure, if he learns how to manage and plan his time, then his work will begin to get completed well before time and he will enjoy success throughout his life.

Some people face failures in their relationships. They are always victims of misunderstandings. People are unable to understand them. In order to overcome this problem, if they learn the importance of communication and the art of expressing themselves clearly, then they will experience the joy of relationships. They will learn the hidden lesson of human relations and start living with everyone lovingly and happily.

A student fails his tests because he always postpones his studies till the eleventh hour. From this failure, if he learns the lesson of getting rid of procrastination and developing the habit of studying regularly, then he will be able to face all his upcoming tests without any stress and achieve success.

If a person has faced some failure and developed the habit of often sinking into depression, then from this attack of depression he can learn the lesson of meditation. How to realize one's true Self? How to surrender oneself in divine devotion, how to surrender stress, problems, and worries to the Almighty? Due to this lesson, he will lead his life in the bliss of divine devotion.

Thus, by learning lessons from every problem in life, you will unravel the diamond of a lesson from the problem and progress further.

THE FIFTH Diamond: A Challenge

Every problem has a challenge within it. When you stagnate in your comfort zone, problems come to shake you up. They pose challenges at you. You might wonder how you can meet these challenges with all your limitations. At such time, counter this thought by questioning yourself, "How can I solve this problem despite these limitations? How can I make this impossible task possible?" With such questioning you open the mind to receive answers. You then accept these challenges, work upon them and soon you will be able to transcend your limitations.

In the board game of carom, you accept the rule of playing by staying between two lines. By using the striker placed between the two limiting lines, you need to pocket the carom coins. In the same way, accept the limitations of your body and derive joy from the challenges that they throw at you.

The limiting lines are not meant to bind you, but rather offer you the opportunities to express your freedom through limitations. In this world there are many people who are deaf, dumb, blind or handicapped in other ways, and face many difficulties. You may be aware that in video games, as you reach the higher levels, the game becomes more challenging. But if you have become an expert, then you willingly and happily take on those challenges and play at the higher levels. Similarly, people with handicaps are higher players. They have chosen to play this earthly game with these extra challenges and are playing at a higher level. If they are reminded of this truth, they can happily take on their challenges and overcome failures. There have been numerous examples of handicapped people who have attained tremendous success.

On the other hand, those who do not have any handicaps should realize that this is a great responsibility upon them. If they are free from all problems, then they should become instrumental in liberating others from their problems. This understanding is important for them that now their responsibility has increased. If you do not have problems in your life, then become responsible and help others to come out of their problems. Express your gratitude to God for not having any problems and accept a new challenge.

In spite of many limitations such as the lack of money, pains of the body, taunts of people, lack of strength, lack of time, spending a lot of time to earn your livelihood, and so on, if you are still able to express your true Self, then you will be called a successful player. In order to become a successful player in the game of life, learn to accept the challenge of your limitations.

When you are able to see every problem as an opportunity and realize your responsibility, accept the challenge, become instrumental for helping others, learn your lessons, climb the ladder and reach the pinnacle of progress, you will not just find the solutions to your problems but also obtain the hidden gift. You will not find any problem to be a problem at all. You will no longer consider any incident to be a problem.

SECTION II

18 SOLUTIONS TO ANY PROBLEM

4

The Little Gita of Problem Solving

In the Indian epic, Mahabharata, Arjuna received the highest wisdom from Lord Krishna in eighteen chapters that formed the Bhagavad Gita. You can read this book further as a little Gita of problem solving! You will receive eighteen solution approaches to all your problems. Whenever you have a problem, go through these solution approaches, find the relevant approach to solve your problem, take a pause and reflect on it to take necessary action.

The eighteen solutions begin with gross approaches that deal with superficial aspects of your problem situations and progressively delve deeper into subtler aspects that transcend the plane where the situation occurs.

Subtler solutions work at a deeper level of our perspectives and approach to life and thus can bring forth a far-reaching effect in our lives. In addition to solving the immediate problem situations we are faced with, these solution approaches also help in preparing ourselves to deal with future life situations in a more effective manner.

It will be helpful to read these solution approaches in the given sequence for the first time. Once you have gathered the eighteen solutions, you can then choose any relevant approach and apply it to your given situation.

Solution 1

Increase Patience

In order to solve any problem, we need to be in the right frame of mind. If our mind is filled with several thoughts, then we will not gather any of the diamonds viz. the solution, the gift, the ladder, the lesson, or the challenge from the problem. The state of mental turmoil can completely delude our focus and blind us, thereby preventing us from seeing the solution clearly. It's like the storm arising out of our thoughts that defiles our mental mirror and does not allow the clear image to get reflected therein. If we try to find a solution when we are entangled in our thoughts, we can possibly complicate even the simplest of situations. At such time, patience is the solution.

Patiently accept the situation as-it-is without resisting it. First allow your mind to calm down and relax. Don't do anything at that time and don't be troubled by the thought of how not to do anything. As the mind calms down, it makes way for the solution to unravel itself. Just like day follows night, the solution to every problem always follows the problem. Let's understand how this mental state is achieved with the help of an example.

When a ship is caught in a storm and is unable to steer through, the captain of the ship releases the anchor of the ship into water. This anchor is used till the time the storm does not recede. This period is the time for doing nothing – the time of unconditional waiting. The captain of the ship waits till the weather becomes clear so that it could again sail safely. If he still sails instead of waiting, then it might overturn and sink.

Similarly, during a problematic situation when a multitude of thoughts arises and clouds your vision and begins to sink the "ship of faith", it is better to choose to wait and do nothing till you receive further indications. At this time you should only witness your thoughts. You should look at the waves of your thoughts from a standpoint of a detached witness. By witnessing thoughts in this manner, you shift your focus away from the problem; the power of negative thoughts weakens. The lost faith begins to reawaken. Such witnessing is a state where one does nothing.

Patience is not a passive trait, where you resign to the situation. On the other hand, patience comes from a position of conviction that the most apt solution will surely emerge in due course of time, provided we wait in a happy natural state without fretting too much about the problem at hand.

Trying to deal with problems by thinking about them and then acting from these thoughts may seem rational. However, when we watch our thoughts in a detached manner, we stop blowing problems out of proportion through our thinking. Patience enables us to step out of our limited thought processes and find solutions that are waiting to emerge intuitively. We begin to realize that most of the problems are actually related to our thoughts or the way we perceive it. The very act of thinking about our problems actually keeps them alive.

In essence, observing the thoughts as a witness is a state of non-action. When thoughts are observed from a distance, they stop getting fueled and eventually die down. Otherwise our mind doesn't want to easily dissociate itself from the thought that it gets attached to.

There are many effective methods of meditation that can help in detaching from thoughts. In order to shift the focus from the problem, every method is of help. At such times, even practicing a simple meditation technique can be of help as the mind is off the problem for that period.

Keeping your eyes closed, you may observe your incoming and outgoing breath. You may watch your thoughts as if they were clouds passing by. You can also perform Self-Enquiry by asking, "Exactly what to whom? This problem has appeared to whom? Who is getting stressed? Who is not able to detach from these disturbing thoughts? Who is not able to shift his focus from the problem? Exactly where is the pain, tension or stress in the body? Where is the pulsation being felt? Where is the vibration being felt that is causing distress?"

At such a time, first make your body taut and then leave it loose. If required, you may lie down in *Shavasana* ("Corpse pose" – a yogic relaxation posture where a person lies down on his back and leaves his body loose like a corpse). Alternatively, you may stretch and relax those parts of your body, which are experiencing discomfort. You may drink ample water, exercise rigorously. You may engage yourself in some creative work with your instinctive mind or even play with children. By doing any of these, you will be able to shift your focus away from the thought of the problem.

You can see that being present in patient stillness is a solution in itself. Once you decide to stay put with this solution for a few days, you will notice new scenes emerging. You will then be happy for having kept patience. It's as if a key of a harmonium has been pressed and you are patiently waiting to get a clear indication when the next key needs to be pressed without any hurry.

Solution 2

Gather Right Information

In the cashless world of e-money, you may have observed that if you are not aware of net banking transactions, you find yourself in trouble. The solution is to get yourself acquainted with it. As you get familiar with the system, you start transacting smoothly. So, what seems to be an ominous problem with cash transactions evaporates when you gain knowledge of electronic commerce.

As another example, if you visit a foreign country and don't know the systems there, you will find yourself constricted and less confident. But the minute you get accustomed to the system, you find yourself very comfortable and you behave as if you have been there since ages.

When you are appointed on a new project, as a novice you observe each and everything going on in the project. But as you get inducted into the project, you gain ease with it and even excel further.

Usually those who are into research assignments have to go through lot of material, visit many faculties. After enormous amount of work, they find themselves not leading anywhere. At such times, they need to remind themselves that they still need to acquire more information.

Some problems persist due to lack of information. When you don't have necessary information, you might face a problematic situation. Once you gather the correct information, you wonder how easy the task was and all your apprehensions begin to fade away. Consider that you could be stuck with a problem in the morning without knowing what to do. Later, during the day you receive a phone call that provides you all the required information. By evening, you may find that you have surpassed the problem. All of these can happen because of right information.

Sometimes, you need to take information from someone else and at some other times you need to search for it on your own. While seeking information from others, you may need to wait patiently. While searching for it on your own, you may need to visit some other places as well. Your mind may grumble and lament during this process. At such times, ask your mind to stop grieving for the sorrow you haven't received in the first place. Educate the mind that you will first receive the information and then lament only if required. Most of the times, you may notice that as you receive the right information, your problem gets solved.

Solution 3

Analyze the Root Cause

For some problems, you need to become a doctor and diagnose the ailment. Doctors perform several tests to identify the primary reason or the root cause of the ailment. The solution can be extremely simple when you locate the main obstacle.

As another example, in companies they conduct post implementation reviews after they complete a project. In this, they carry out a root cause analysis to see which factors delayed the deadline. Then they work upon it to improve their performance in the next delivery cycle.

When you get to know the obstacle on your way, you can easily circumvent it. However, in some cases, the obstacle is not identified correctly, and your whole attention revolves around something unimportant. Naturally you wonder that despite putting all the effort, the desired outcome is not achieved. You make 80% effort but get only 20% results. In this situation, you should use the 80-20 principle to exactly locate the root cause of your problem.

80-20 principle

The 80-20 principle helps you focus your energies only on important tasks. It teaches you to focus on those 20% jobs that give you the maximum results – 80% results. According to this principle every task has a 20% part, which is vital and 80%, which is relatively less important.

80% of our energy must be invested in such tasks which will contribute to the development of our home, family, ourselves and our society. But we invest 80% of our energy in such kind of activities, that make us feel at the end of the day, that only 20% of our tasks were accomplished. We must actually carry out those 20% of our activities that can genuinely have 80% significance in our lives.

Let's understand this with the help of few examples. A home maker while cooking uses salt, which is only 20% of the spices. But if the remaining 80% ingredients were added and cooked without the 20% salt, the food would remain tasteless and will not be preferred for consumption by many.

Similarly, when we talk about friends and relatives, it is only 20% who are truly close friends or relatives, who contribute to 80% of contentment in your life. The others are but only acquaintances and are not as important in your life and have a 20% impact on your life.

For solving a problem, first analyze and identify the 20% critical tasks of a problem, which gives 80% of effective results and then invest your energies first on those 20% critical tasks which will actually help in solving the problem. If this 20% is not accomplished, it will cause complications.

Suppose that you have a problem with your job. You don't feel satisfied at your job. As a result, you lack motivation to persevere with the job. When you analyze the root cause using 80-20 principle, you find that your company has great sales figures but it works less on subtler aspects like goodwill and customer trust.

In this case, 80% factor is the sales figure and 20% factor is the goodwill and customer trust. Even if you work hard on the 80% factor, it yields only 20% results. If you start working on the 20% factor, 80% of your work will be achieved. You will feel satisfied and the customer satisfaction will also improve. As you gain a sense of completeness and fulfillment, you will then feel it worth devoting your time to such a job.

When you focus your entire energy on 20% vital tasks from your daily list then 80% results are assured. For example, does physical exercises constitute the 20% of your daily jobs or the 80%? If it is 20%, then you will need to consider investing time for exercises. You are clearly aware that 20% collectively from exercises and diet contributes to 80% vital result – Health. Instead of waiting for this advice from the doctor, it will be helpful to begin exercises today.

Whenever you feel you are wasting time, remind yourself about the 20% vital tasks that require your complete focus. You can prioritize and optimize the utilization of your time by identifying, defining and focusing on the 20% essential tasks of your day.

Fine thinking

Once you identify the 20% area on which you need to focus in order to achieve 80% of results, deeply reflect on the subtler details of that area without ignoring even a minor point, however tangential it may be. For this, you may use the 5W technique – what, why, how, who and when.

If you are thinking about a goal or a project, you can break it down into sequential steps that lead to the desired result. Each step can be broken down into sub-steps. For each step, you can contemplate on the following aspects –

1. The significance and purpose of the given task.
2. The skills and competency required to carry out the task.
3. The governing factors or dependencies for its effective completion.
4. The pre-requisites or pre-conditions required for entering into the process.
5. The post-requisites or exit-criteria required for moving from one task to the other.

Thus, you can approach your problem from various angles, which may not have been thought of earlier. It helps reveal hidden aspects that you would otherwise have never known.

Solution 4

Work Vigorously for a Few Days

For some problems you fail to realize that it only requires a few days of hard work to solve them. Let's assume that you need to complete an assignment. Initially, it might seem to be a huge task. So, quite naturally the mind may grumble, "Oh, there's so much of work to be done. I don't know when all this can be accomplished. It's a big problem." The mind knows that if it starts working at it, it will have to work relentlessly. By grumbling this way, it tries to find an excuse to escape from the task.

When the mind protests and screams hoarse about the problem, it seems difficult to start with the solution. At this juncture, tell yourself, "I have to work hard for two to three days. This is the solution to my problem." As you decide to make a start and work vigorously for two to three days, a part of the problem is already solved and the remaining part will begin to fall into place. Thus, by completing one part of the problem, you help the next scene to unfold whereby the entire problem will move towards complete solution.

Certain problems need regular attention whereas for certain other problem situations, vigorous action is warranted for some days. Though it won't be totally solved at the outset, it can gradually move towards the solution. When one part gets solved, the next one appears.

Solution 5

Persevere and Persist

There are certain kinds of problems for which you need to work persistently. If you have health related issues then you ought to do exercises daily, practice *pranayama*, and inculcate some healthy food habits so that you can regain your health. If you work on it for some time and then drop it in between, again start working on it, you will find that the health problem still persists. It has not moved to resolution.

So it is with habits like smoking or alcohol. Some people try very hard to get rid of these habits but are not able to, due to lack of perseverance.

There are some problems which demand consistent attention and perseverance. Unfortunately, people begin to work on them but stop after a few days, then they again start and again stop. This cycle goes on for years. They do everything that is required and also follow all the steps, but for want of persistence, the desired results are not achieved.

You may have seen that many sportsmen reach the pinnacle of success in their chosen sport. However, a rare few manage to remain at the top and sustain their performance over many years. Their secret lies in perseverance.

There are some people who attain name, fame and success overnight but cannot sustain at the helm for long. After a few days, they again slide back to where they were. This happens because they lack perseverance.

When we break good practices, we tend to slide backwards instead of making progress. Persistence and consistency are the hallmark to success. Problems move towards resolution when we begin to work at them with perseverance.

Solution 6

Revisit Your Goal

If a frog is thrown into a bucket of boiling hot water, it will instantly jump out. However, if the same frog is put in cold water, which is then gradually heated, it will remain and boil to death. This is because the frog cannot sense the gradual rise in the water temperature.

So it is with us humans. Most of us easily notice sudden, obvious changes that occur in our everyday life. However, very few are able to notice the gradual and subtle changes that occur at a snail's pace in the longer term.

Usually, we carry out our activities unquestioningly, just as we always do. The parameters that govern our lives keep changing over time. As a result, the conditions that we based our earlier decisions on need not necessarily be applicable now.

There is always room for improvement, fine-tuning, and reorientation in whatever we do. Hence, we need to pause frequently and re-think. We need to determine whether we should continue to follow the same course of action that we had earlier, or make suitable corrections.

Besides external factors, there may also be internal drivers for re-looking our goals. Everything is constantly changing, not just in our environment, but also within us. Over a period of time, our understanding can change; our perception of life itself can undergo a complete transformation.

As our perceptions, values, and understanding changes, we must re-evaluate our aims. We may have to re-assess the reasons why and how we do the things we do. Perhaps the aims that we set for ourselves are no longer relevant, given our redefined purposes. We may need to re-align our approach with what gives us fulfillment now. If we do not contemplate and re-assess our approach to life from time to time, we invite frustration and discontentment into our life.

Certain problem situations come to make us re-think our goals. If you haven't set your goal as yet, do it now. However, if you have already set a goal for yourself, revisit it. The more you revisit your goal, the more you will strengthen the likelihood of its actualization. Revisiting your goal again and again helps you attune with it. It also boosts your backup power.

The more you revisit your goal, the more you become aware of its finer and subtler details. You become aware of what you exactly want in your life. It is just like when you visit a temple for the first time, you may notice certain things. On your subsequent visits, you observe new things that you hadn't noticed earlier. Thus, with every visit, you are enriched with information and your clarity rises. Thus, revisit your goal again and again, fine-tune it with subtler details, and know exactly what you really want.

Solution 7

Change Your Perspective

There are several problems that can be solved by a mere change of perspective. You only need to change your attitude and do nothing else. When you look deeper at your perspective towards a particular problem, you will begin to gain insights into any limitations in the way you are seeing the situation. You get to know that your line of thought needs to be changed and you ought to adopt a positive outlook. This is because you could have been stuck with a negative outlook till then.

At this time, note down whatever comes to your mind. Writing your thoughts on paper helps to empty unnecessary mental clutter and create space for new ideas and new possibilities to emerge. This sparks your true creativity and you start thinking out of box. You break out of fixed ways of thinking. As you stretch your mind to its limits, your latent creative potential gets activated. It is then that the most amazing, inspiring and ingenious ideas spring forth.

When you write down the problem statement, it makes it possible to redefine it. When you redefine the problem statement, it can turn out that there's no problem, or perhaps the problem is not as grave as it seemed. Redefining the problem helps us gain a perspective shift. For example, if the problem presents itself as "This person is so difficult. I can't come to terms with him." You can redefine it as, "This person does not seem to align with how I wish to see him." This opens your mind to focus on your expectations for him and reconsider them.

In order to change your perspective, you can also ask yourself, "Am I the first person in the world to have faced this problem?" After that, contemplate on the answer to this question. Whenever you think of your troubled situation, remember that such a problem has certainly arisen earlier in the lives of many people. Imagine how they would have handled this problem.

Suppose you have relationship issues and believe that others are responsible for these issues; that they have to change. You need to tell yourself, "This situation is exactly what I need for this moment." Now start giving your mind evidences about how these issues in relationships have arisen to suit your need. By doing this, you change your perspective, paving the way to a solution. You will find that by not cooperating with you, people are actually helping you to inculcate higher qualities like patience, courage, compassion and proficiency in communication within you. They are playing a key role in your life. They are your co-creators.

If someone is irritating you, it can be considered that they are helping you to increase your patience. If you are faced with a fearful incident, understand that it has come to strengthen you and raise your courage. If by looking at someone you are developing hatred, understand that he is helping you to develop compassion within.

If you believe that a person is useless, should he be made useful or should you change your perspective? It's impossible to change everyone to suit your likes. Instead it's easier to change your perspective. You can tell yourself, "This is exactly what I need for this moment." You will develop a new perspective that even those people who do not seem to be of any use have a role in your life, albeit of a slightly different nature, which may not be visible to you right now. They may be serving as mirrors to show you your own limited beliefs. By being with them, you get to witness the feelings that they evoke within you. Feelings of anger, irritability, hatred, jealousy, etc. may come to light.

Only when such negative vices come to light will you be made aware of what lies within you. Only then you will think of getting rid of them. At the same time, the so-called useless person helps you develop vital qualities like patience, self-control and discipline within you. If the seemingly useless people make you aware of your negative aspects and help you develop the positive qualities within you, then how can they be useless?!

Thus, everything in the world is useful, nothing is useless, not even the useless. Once, you gain this paradigm shift in your perspective, you will say, "He is a very useful person. In fact, he is just right for the work he is doing." By merely changing your perspective, the same situation, which used to upset you, will now make you happy. You will thank those people from the bottom of your heart.

Many a time, we tend to work on only those problems that trouble us. Consider that problems occur in your life so that you will do some investigation and research on it, which will help several others handle similar situations in the future. In fact, everybody in this world has been given some problem or the other.

When we personalize our problems, we limit our perspective and get entangled in negativity. When we treat the problem impersonally as a springboard for human progress, we rise beyond limitations and become receptive to solutions. People who are bestowed with problems are destined to carry out some specific responsibilities too, in future. If you come to know that responsibility beforehand, then you would not have any tension whatsoever.

We can see how Helen Keller turned her problem into an opportunity and became instrumental for mass uplift of physically challenged people in the world. Helen Keller was a blind, deaf, and dumb girl who grew up to become a popular motivational speaker and writer. Have you ever imagined how this miracle could have happened? Even today she is the source of inspiration for thousands of blind students – if Helen Keller could achieve such marvels despite her physical disability, so can they. Today one can see that Helen Keller's handicap was destined to be the beacon light for many others.

When you look at the problem with the right understanding you come to know that the problem, which you are considering to be yours, is not at all yours. You have been given a problem so that you will become instrumental to solve the problem for thousands of others. You will then take it as a challenge to solve the problem. Solving your problem will become a means for serving others. If a person suffered from an incurable disease and ultimately discovered a medicine, not only did he cure himself, but also thousands of others from the disease. Thus, his problem became a boon for everyone. Otherwise, without the right understanding, you get attached to the problem and fail to overcome it.

All of us have come to earth with the grand purpose of fulfilling some of our responsibilities. Until we perform them we will not feel content. Hence, consider all the problems that you encounter as opportunities to progress; contemplate and rethink over them. Rise beyond the limited individualistic view and consider your problems from an impersonal standpoint. Do not unnecessarily implore by considering your problems to be merely your "personal" ones.

Solution 8

Identify the Unexpected

The journey of life abounds in uncertainties. We often come across situations, which we wouldn't expect. You may have no idea that a particular person would behave in a particular manner, or that things would turn out in a particular way. Often unexpected happenings are not acceptable. For example, your promotion at the workplace might be blocked or delayed.

For such problems that arise unexpectedly, you need to identify the element that occurred unexpectedly, or which could perhaps occur in the future. Why do you need to identify the unexpected? It is because if you are not clear about your destination, you will be put on the right track with the help of these unexpected incidents. They force you to think differently and laterally.

Actually, these unexpected incidents are positive harbingers of growth. They indicate that there are certain important things that are incomplete and need to be completed first. It also means that the desired preparations are not done. They indicate that you are not well equipped with the qualities and knowledge required to reach your destination. Therefore, when some unexpected scenes occur, it is time to rejoice, considering it as a game with the unknown; it is an effort to fix the missing links.

In a jigsaw puzzle, if you put a piece at the wrong place, you get stuck and can't proceed. It means something unexpected has happened and you need to take that piece out and put it at its correct place. Life is a continuous jigsaw game with the unknown. If you fix a piece at the correct place, you get "good" vibes; and conversely when you fix the piece at the wrong place, you receive "bad" vibes. Sometimes, these unexpected events make you rethink your strategies and plans.

Again, when you revise your goal, you actually make a new picture. Then if anything unexpected happens, you become astonished. For example, you might not expect help from a certain person, but help is accorded to you and a new channel is opened. You are surprised. Similarly, suppose you had planned to study or watch TV in the evening. However, you return home to find unexpected guests. Don't sulk but soar high with the unexpected. There are some surprises in store for you, accept them gracefully, with a smile.

If you have to reach somewhere urgently and you get stuck in a traffic jam, understand that it has come to fix the piece in the jigsaw puzzle at the right place. Maybe you are required to learn patience or rethink and reflect over the matter in the pause provided to you before you reach the venue. Thus, you don't know what's in store for you in the unseen. This delay comes to unfold some hitherto unknown scenes in your life. As you realize this, you can remain calm even in that externally stressful situation.

Similarly, when there is loss of money, or you or your loved one gets afflicted by an incurable disease, or you have an argument with your neighbor, instead of spending time in brooding over your so-called distress, you would utilize that time in studying the lessons of life.

You become courageous only after you pass through crisis. Till the time you get this lesson completely ingrained in your mind, tension, fear, and crises will continue to haunt you. You would value love only when you have seen hatred. When you learn to gracefully play with the unknown, you would be able to identify the "gift of nature" that lies beneath every crisis.

Understand that the crises appear not to bog us down, but to push us forward on the path of success. Invariably, the fear of an unexpected crisis is much more than the severity of the crisis itself! If you face your testing time with the understanding that it has come to help you reach the goal of your life, you would be able to comfortably overcome that crisis situation. In this manner, you can convert every unexpected situation into an opportunity to strengthen you.

Solution 9

Sow the Seed of Faith

For some problems, you have to only sow the seed of faith. The seeds that you sow bear fruit, which is multiplied many times over. This is because nature returns every seed multiplied a several times over – be it your goodness or badness. This is the law of nature. Nature gives everything in abundance.

While you are going through a problem, you help many others who have similar problems with the belief that you are sowing the seed of faith. This seed of faith brings forth the solution to your problem. Your problem gets solved in the process. When you give, you demonstrate your faith and gratitude for the free-flow of abundance.

Thus, every day find ways to give, to share what you have. When you are grateful for what you have, you give it to others – be it money, time, support, encouragement. If you feel you don't have enough of something, start giving that! By giving gratefully and continuously, you place yourself in the free-flow of life and become a channel for abundance to work through you. By giving, you demonstrate your gratitude in action for what you have and also what you don't! You get into a frame of receptivity and attract the highest possibilities into your life.

If you are without a job, you can help many others who are jobless. As they secure jobs, you too will get employed in the process. If you are sick and feel the need that people should empathize with you, then you need to seize the initiative to empathize with what others are feeling or going through. This act of empathy on your part will give you joy and contentment.

If you are in need of money, you can sow the seed of faith by helping someone who is in need. Your need will in turn be fulfilled. If you give your ear to someone, you too will be given attention. If you serve someone, you too will be served when the time will come. If you play an active role in someone's development, your development is assured.

Solution 10

Reframe Your Self-talk

In case of some problems, you only need to reframe what you keep telling yourself. For example, when the mind is consumed by negative thoughts and constantly repeating that whatever is happening is not good or that it is putting you in trouble, you need to simply reframe your self-talk with sentences such as: "Everything is happening in perfect order as per my divine plan" or "I am not going to die before my actual death." Such positively reframed statements will work miracles. Once you reframe the sentences that you keep telling yourself, you will realize that you were worrying merely because of the negative thoughts that kept inundating your awareness or considering death even before its time.

There will be different sentences for different situations. When your mind starts describing some pessimistic situation and makes you believe it to be real, at such junctures, you need to insert these positive sentences in between. For example, suppose that the mind warns you, "This person is afflicted by this particular disease; it can happen to me too." At that juncture, reframe your sentence and tell the mind, "Do you know what he has prayed for? If you don't know, then be silent. Not everyone faces the same consequences. Your thoughts and self-talk determine what will happen with you."

Thus, for some problems you need to counter your mind's negative talk with the repetition of positive self-talk. That's the only thing you need to do as long as the problem persists. In fact, that's the very purpose of the practice of chanting in spirituality. You keep chanting some holy words from a sacred text, the name of God, some mantra, or some positive affirmations until it gets hardwired in your brain and determines how your mind functions. Your mind begins to chant those sentences on its own. Further, you need not have to always chant them aloud. You can utter them mentally as well.

Initially, you have to make conscious effort to inculcate this habit of chanting positive sentences or words. You need to practice repeating it to such an extent that just by uttering the word once, your mind should continue chanting it internally on its own. Unless this happens, introducing positive thoughts amidst the negative ones is impossible. This is because our outer mind is externally directed. It probes the details of the problem time and again. Instead of focusing on the positive aspects in your life, it tends to focus on what's going wrong in your life. It can magnify the problem and can even convince you that nothing is working out well in your life. The habit of chanting comes handy at such times.

It helps to cultivate the habit of chanting well in advance so that when situations arise, you can combat them by chanting positive statements automatically. You can even chant sentences like "Thy will is my will", "Let love, joy, and peace rule my life", "What's above all these problems? Love, joy, and peace." Keep chanting such words or sentences that give you a positive shift of perspective.

Solution 11

Convert Hurt to Humor

Some problems have their root in the sense of feeling hurt. More than the loss of money, time or effort, it is the resultant sense of feeling hurt that poses the real problem. For such problems, you need to first raise your level of awareness and solve the problem from this elevated level of awareness. This is because problems can never be truly solved at the same level of awareness that they were created in.

With higher awareness comes clarity, which enables you to perceive the situation in a new light. This higher perception, in itself, serves to move the problem towards its natural resolution. For this, you need to learn the art of converting the hurtful feeling into humor.

Convert the feeling of hurt to humor deliberately till the problem persists. A student who had scored only 5 in 100 in his exams was laughing. The teacher asked him why he was laughing. He replied that there must have been some error in checking or grading his answers, as all his answers were incorrect. So he didn't deserve even 5 marks; his result could have been worse.

A man built his mansion and the day he was going to shift to his mansion, the mansion collapsed. Everyone felt very bad for this man, but were surprised to see this man distributing sweets to everyone and saying that whatever happens is only for good. When he was asked, he told that if the mansion were to fall after his family had moved in, it would have been such a great loss for him. But now his family is safe and secure.

Seeing things in a lighter vein does not mean that we are being careless or unwilling to improve the situation. When we crack jokes, we come out of the limited negative mindset that stops solutions from reaching us. We need to learn to laugh at situations, no matter how ominous they may seem. This is an important lesson. Whatever happens to us, serves to transport us to the next higher level of awareness, for our development and spiritual growth. Nothing ever happens to drag us backward. Never have an iota of doubt. Nature is always leading us forward to progress in the journey of life.

It is a matter of exhilaration that nature always pushes us to the next higher level. When you aspire to reach an exalted state, the real Self compliments you through a noble feeling that you sense. When our thoughts resonate with others, we compliment the person. When we are not in sync with the nature's plan for progress, we experience a hurtful feeling.

Feelings are the language of the real Self. The real Self communicates with us through this subtle language of feelings. We need to invest our time in learning this subtle language of the Self. The moment a negative feeling comes to the mind, we start complaining and cursing instead of taking a cue from it. A negative feeling is only conveying that we are falling out of alignment with nature's grand plan for our progress. A peaceful and joyous feeling conveys that we are on the right track.

When you covert the hurt to humor, your feelings change and that's where the miracle begins. You begin to synchronize with the real Self within you. You need to do this deliberately as long as the problem persists. When you witness its positive effect, you may choose to continue doing it thereafter.

When you wish ill for others, you get a bad feeling. It's nothing but the indication from the Self that you are not thinking right. This feeling does not come in the form of words or through an Oracle. It comes from within through the medium of the feelings that you sense. When a person deviates in the wrong direction, he needs to be goaded to the right one. This goading is nothing but guiding him. However, he might feel that he is being pushed, mistreated and subjected to injustice; because he doesn't have the perspective of the entire development.

This step involves a deliberate thinking – a thinking that is opposite to what is normally thought in situations. You can shift the hurtful feeling to one of humor by asking yourself an awakening question – "Do I choose to take this situation as a wound that disappoints me, or a joke in the divine plan of life meant to uplift me?" Asking this question can raise your level of awareness and enable you to transmute the hurtful feeling into one of humor.

Solution 12

Identify the Obstacle Wall

Before we go ahead with this solution, let's first examine some problem situations.

- You aspire to become an eloquent speaker. You want to address people from the stage and share your thoughts. However, you are gripped with stage fright.

- You wish to become a renowned writer but don't feel like taking all that effort to meet up with your commitments.

- You wish to become an expert in a particular area of scientific research. However, when you face challenging situations, you start feeling that you are a misfit.

- You wish to ace your exams, but when you start solving your exam paper, you are seized by the fear of failure.

- You wish to become a soft and cordial person, but when you see that people do not meet your expectations, you become angry.

What do these problems suggest? They suggest that there is an obstacle in whatever you want to achieve in life. For some problems, you need to identify this obstacle wall that exists between you and your goal of life. You may find this obstacle wall posing a roadblock, much against your wishes. No one would want any obstacles in their path to success.

You may wonder why this obstacle wall is placed on the way to success at the first place. It is because those who are determined to surpass this wall will do so. Only they are destined to succeed, others are not. This wall comes on the way to test those who are not strong willed. There are certain spots on this obstacle wall, which are relatively weak. Those who really wish to surmount this obstacle wall, have to simply tap these spots and make headway, while others remain stranded by this seemingly formidable obstacle. They find it easier to give up by quoting various excuses for not being able to surpass the wall. No sooner does the obstacle come in sight, than they begin to shudder with various apprehensions.

It is important to identify that obstacle and ask yourself how badly you long to achieve your objective, your goal that exists across the obstacle wall. Introspect whether your resolve to achieve your aim in life is indeed strong enough or it is merely a lukewarm wish that withers at the slightest peril? If you indeed want success, you would locate the weak spot on the obstacle wall. By removing it, you will be able to do away with the entire wall. This is the law of nature.

In order to locate the weak spot, you need to challenge your assumptions. It could be possible that the so-called problem may not be there at the first place. Your assumptions may be leading you to perceive the situation as a problem. For example, if you believe a pancake to be always round and find a square pancake, you might perceive it as a problem. As you challenge your assumption, the problem no longer exists.

Similarly, you perceive the situation to be a problem and the tests, stress coming along with it as obstacles. But conversely, tests, stress, and problems appear in our lives only to make us progress. They trigger our development. However, due to lack of right understanding, we identify them as obstacles. Consider the problems of your life as tests that are arranged to make you introspect whether whatever you have learnt so far is helping you to progress further. Then you would not consider the problems as problems, but rather as stepping-stones to march ahead towards your goal.

Henceforth, when you are faced with a problem, ask yourself whether you are going to buckle down. As you face the problem, you will find yourself emerging stronger. You will build faith that the problem is not meant to pull you down, but to make you stronger. In other words, the problem that cannot crush you only makes you bolder when you face it. You emerge a winner. With this understanding, you would notice that all those trifles, which used to bother you earlier won't do so anymore and you will learn from every situation of life.

With this understanding, if you revisit the above-mentioned problems, you will find that each of them demands certain qualities to be developed within you in order to excel in the respective fields. However fierce the problems may appear, treat them as opportunities. If you don't wither away, the problems will. On their way out of your life, problems will strengthen your faith and conviction and lead you on the path of progress. However, if you are shaken by the problems, the problems persist and prevent you from attaining your goal. If you are really sure that you want to achieve your goal, no matter what, then you will transcend these obstacles and go beyond, you will develop those qualities.

Thus, if you want to become an eloquent speaker, there is a higher purpose behind the existence of stage fright. Those who are destined to address huge audiences are not cowed down by this fear; rather they win over these obstacles and march forward. They learn the precious lesson of manifesting courage when they are faced with fears within them. There are many, who may want to become eloquent speakers, but in practicality, very few people overcome stage fright. Had this not been so and had everybody been rid of stage fright, then we would have more speakers than listeners!

If you want to become a renowned writer, you need to cross the obstacle of lethargy. Only then can you make progress. The challenging commitments come to test whether you are indeed serious about your passion.

If you wish to become an expert in research, you can't afford to lose your spirits and get stranded in between. You need to face the challenges with perseverance. Equip yourself with the requisite skills in order to meet these challenges.

Make the fear of failure a stepping-stone to ace your exams. Understand that fear has come to get some work done through you. You will then take your studies seriously and progress further.

If you wish to become a soft and cordial person, learn to win over your anger. As you win over your anger, you will have harmonious relations with people as a bonus.

Solution 13

Retain the Happy Hat and Be in Gratitude

The owner of a circus had pitched his circus tent on the outskirts of the city. Just a day before the show, there came a violent storm that blew away the tent.

The circus owner was a veteran who had seen the rough of life. While the members of the troupe were running helter-skelter, worrying how they will put up the show, the trapeze artist caught sight of the owner walking around with an enigmatic smile.

Seeing his smile of assurance, the trapeze artist told the others, "I have seen our boss smile; I don't think we need to be worried. Let's go and talk to him." They approached him, asking what they should be doing next.

Before instructing them on how to salvage the weathered tent, he gave them a very important message: "The tent may have blown away, but hold onto your happy hat, lest you lose that too… the show is far from over!"

So it is with our lives too. There are situations that appear in our lives and completely shake us up. It is natural to feel as if all the miseries of the world have befallen us. What should we do in such situations?

Though it may not have been possible to hold onto the roof of the tent, at least hold tight onto your hat. The storm has blown away your roof and the negative thoughts that arise thereafter can also take away your hat. The mind would think of all the loss that has occurred, like the rent paid for the tent has gone down the drain, the rain may start pouring anytime, etc. Such negative thoughts blow away your happiness or happy hat.

When calamities come, they may seem to ravage our surroundings, but the least we can do in these circumstances is to hold onto our happy hat. No matter what problems arise in your life, ask yourself, "Has my happy hat blown off?" Catch hold of it. If your happy hat has gone, then the reconstruction of your roof becomes more difficult. If you keep your happy hat intact, you can construct a concrete roof. The old roof blew away because the new roof had to come. If some changes occur in your life, remember that there is a replacement going on. New scenes are going to come in your life. As we are not aware of what's going to happen next in our life, we try to resist the situation. However, if we remain happy amidst all situations of our life, we help the next scene to unfold. Who knows, the next scene could be better than the previous one like the concrete roof in this example!

Thus, for some problems where you can't help the situation, just retain your happy hat. You may find it difficult to be happy in such perilous and sorrowful situations. In order to retain your happy hat, you may either watch a comedy show, or go on a nature trail, listen to something that makes you delighted. Start gathering your hat of happiness and count your blessings. Record the feelings of gratitude, because many a times we tend to forget the good things that happened in our lives as we are always overburdened by our problems. However, we do not fail to dwell on the negative things that occur in our life.

Being in gratitude loosens the grip of negative feelings. Our focus shifts from scarcity to boundless abundance. Abundance then begins to show up in our life. When we abide in the state of joy regardless of circumstances, we become a magnet that attracts the most suitable solutions to our problems. With the feeling of happiness, especially during sorrowful situations, you transmit happy vibrations to nature. Due to this, nature gives you more experiences of happiness. When you send out vibrations of sorrow, nature creates similar situations where you experience more of sorrow.

Gratitude has immense power. If you are grateful about everything in life, you automatically and constantly focus on the best. You remain in the state of harmony which makes you receptive to the unfolding of your highest possibilities. You break through all limitations in your thinking, and invoke the divine qualities within you. You automatically move away from doubts, worries, and the feeling of scarcity.

Solution 14

Increase Your Backup Power

In our daily lives, we are generally caught up with everyday activities in a way that most of us seldom find time to introspect and re-think our values, our principles and our goals. We make key decisions about how we intend to progress in various facets of life, about the kind of life we would love to lead. But the biggest problem is that all this remains a fantasy only in our minds. We seldom find enough time to write about what we aspire for, about how we have decided to live each day, and why.

The result of this is stress, disharmony, frustration, health problems, and a general lack of clarity that reflects in everyday situations. We don't achieve anything productive when we keep vacillating in our heads about what we really need and why.

However, when we note down the details about what we plan to do, about what our deepest intentions are, and why we would like to live the way we wish to, we will begin to experience a newfound peace and clarity. Putting down our thoughts on paper helps us empty the unnecessary mental clutter and create space for new ideas and new possibilities to emerge.

If you have given a clear picture to nature on what you want to achieve in your life, your vision and goal and have contemplated on it, then nature takes out the next scene from that backup store and presents it to you. If you've not defined anything in your mental backup store, nature gets confused as to what exactly you want from your life. When a problem arises, nature delves in your past and fetches one of the choices made by you. Although they have been outdated solutions, nature can't help it, because you haven't replenished your reserve store with new choices.

In your everyday life, you are continuously watching the world, you are interacting with people, watching TV programs, reading news. By imbibing this information, which often happens to be negative, you are unknowingly increasing the load of undesirable things in your life. In order to maintain a balanced state of love, joy and peace despite this load, you need to increase your backup in the same proportion.

You can change your thoughts and thereby train your focus to create a desired reality. This is because before anything manifests in the physical reality it is first created in thoughts. So you can define what you truly want through your clear thoughts and thus strengthen the backup power of your life.

While leading through various situations of life, certain problems make you unhappy. Problems force you to reflect upon what you truly want in your life. Until you are faced with those situations, you tend to be unaware of what you truly want. But when these problem situations knock at your door, you are forced to work upon your backup, to clearly outline what you truly want in life and give conscious inputs to nature.

The Faith Fair Book

The Faith Fair Book is a backup tool that helps you gain clarity about what you really want in life and why. It is like your personal companion, that will accompany you every day, every moment, reminding you about your life choices, your key decisions, the principles that you live by. You can write details in the Faith Fair Book about how exactly you wish to lead your life.

Writing down your goal in precise detail increases the probability of getting there faster. When your thoughts are placed carefully on paper with full faith, such writing serves as a key tool to aid in the manifestation. What you write down after contemplation goes deep within your mind. You lend your conscious attention to it. This also helps in arousing positive feelings about the goal.

Writing down your goals in precise detail is also the most effective way to gain clarity of what you truly want. Clearly knowing what you want, why you want, and when you want helps you to evaluate whether you are on track, or if you have strayed away from your chosen life path.

By writing the Faith Fair Book, your subconscious mind gets programmed positively. The Universe is convinced that you are indeed sincere and committed to what you really want. It is one way of communicating to nature that you really wish for what you have written.

You get inspired about your goals when you write the Faith Fair Book. This is because your hands, eyes and brain concentrate simultaneously and harmoniously. As a result, the image of what you want is embedded deep within your inner mind, leading to positive results.

When your goal is unclear or muddled, your thoughts tend to meander into unproductive channels, thereby dissipating your time and energy. When your goal is clearly laid out before you, you save time. Your energy starts flowing in your chosen direction. This also improves your confidence, because the Faith Fair Book imparts firmness to your thoughts and raises your willpower.

Mere writing is not enough, unless what you have written is reinforced through consistent reading. Read the list of your goals three to four times a week, and activate your creative powers. Spend some time reflecting on the list. Go through it in full faith with a feeling of fulfilment. Close your eyes and imagine each goal as if you have achieved it. Take a pause to feel what it is like to have achieved the goal. Stay in this feeling of fulfilment for some time.

You can create backup for all 5 aspects of your life viz. physical, mental, social, financial and spiritual. Here are a few examples, which you may include in your backup plan.

1. Backup plan for the physical plane:
   - I want to gain complete health so that I can take giant strides towards success in my chosen field.
   - I want to exercise regularly so that my immunity improves. My healthy body becomes an instrument for the expression of the divine qualities of God.
   - I want to nourish myself with healthy food so that all my body parts function well. I can be fit and fine till the very end.
   - I take proper rest so that I feel energetic and enthusiastic all the time. The efficiency and capacity of my body increases.

2. Backup plan for the mental plane:
   - I consciously choose positive thoughts in my life so that I am receptive for the highest and the best things of life.

My thoughts help everyone around me to create a simple but powerful life.

- I easily adopt various skills so that I become productive and efficient in my work. I teach others who are in need.
- I am free from all bad habits so that I experience the immense joy of the natural flow of abundance in my life. I bloom and blossom in every situation. I can explore my highest potential.

3. Backup plan for the social plane:
   - I have healthy relationship with everyone so that we help each other in growing together.
   - I complete all my tasks on time smoothly so that I enjoy a good balance between my personal and professional life, thus becoming more peaceful and happy.
   - I have committed and loyal colleagues in my office so that we create better products and services in our field of work so as to spread happiness in the world.

4. Backup plan for the financial plane:
   - I always have enough money so that I feel relaxed in money matters and can focus on the ultimate purpose of my life.
   - I always find right options of investment so that there is plenty of money flow in my life. I can help the underprivileged.

5. Backup plan for the spiritual plane:
   - I receive divine guidance so that I always remain connected to the Source of life. I attain the ultimate purpose of life.

- I pray and practice meditation every day so that I tune myself to the divinity within.
- I always live in the present moment so that I enjoy every moment of life fully. I am completely aware of every moment.
- I wish for a world where there is abundance of everything for everyone, so that everyone lives in love, bliss and peace. Everyone attains the highest wisdom and fulfilment.

Additionally, you can also observe the positive qualities in people and tell nature that you want to nurture these positive qualities within you. You want to imbibe the positivity that you see around you. Thus, you make your backup stronger with every situation.

Solution 15

Prayer and Meditation

Sometimes, it can so happen that you are unable to clearly see the solution in its entirety. You only see a part of the solution when you are enmeshed in the bondage created due to mixed emotions. At such times, it helps to use the Pyramid process. Pyramid is an internal cleansing process that comprises of Prayer and Meditation. In this process, you first perform prayers and then sit in meditation. Through meditation, you reach a state where everything is calm, clear and relaxed. Your disturbing thoughts are silenced and you get to clearly see the riverbed of the mind after the thought currents have settled down. You reach a safe plane and then consider what can happen at the most. The solution will automatically emerge from within. This is the magic of Pyramid.

The Power of Prayer

Prayer is such a power, which solves not only physical and mental ailments, but also gets rid of obstacles in the path of spiritual progress. You can pray to a higher source of power – it could be God, Guru, the Higher Self, Consciousness, Creator, or any other spiritual form that you venerate and have faith on. A prayer bears its result when the intensity of faith with which it is rendered is steadfast. It is only faith that matters in case of prayer; not the time or place where it is offered. A prayer can be offered wherever and whenever your faith is evoked.

When you pray with conviction, you basically ask for something, as if you are placing an order for it. With prayer, your desired object begins to move into your life, but you need to be prepared to receive it. If you are unaware of the way prayers work in the unseen, you may unintentionally contradict your prayers through opposing thoughts or even stop praying. This will halt your desired object midway. After some days, when you resume your prayer with renewed faith, the object of your prayer again resumes its journey towards you. As you stop and start your prayer in between, a considerable time is lost in the process. On the contrary, if you sit in meditation immediately after prayer, you are helping the solution to arrive smoothly in harmony, without any hurdle. As a result, the solution emerges shortly. If prayer is the question, meditation is where you receive the answer.

Whenever you are distressed with any problem, know that even before the adversity appeared in your life, you have been already provided its solution. Even before a child is born, nature has made the provision for its food in the form of milk. So, when the problem occurs, you only have to search for the necessary solution, which is hidden somewhere in the problem itself. Prayer only helps in discovering that hidden solution; it makes you receptive to unravel the solution that already exists.

Instead of making use of such a powerful weapon called prayer, which is certainly within our reach, out of sheer despair and ignorance we tend to cling to our egos. Hence, it is advised to always pray first, whenever you are stuck with a problem. Prayer is the highest power given to humans, and we should make use of that power. At a time, when you are completely bewildered and can't think of anything else, you can at least pray.

Watching Your Thoughts – A Meditation Practice

Once you perform prayer, sit in meditation in order to attune yourself so as to receive the result of your prayer. Here is a powerful meditation to help you access inner silence. Consider spending five minutes actually practicing it after reading the instructions that follow.

The key process of this exercise is to de-focus from the content of thoughts by letting them pass by and saying "Next." This way, you allow thoughts to pass by so that they do not hold your attention.

Close your eyes and watch your thoughts as they pass by.

Don't judge them. Simply observe them as they continually pass by. Watch as thoughts come and go. Allow this to occur. Let them continue in a normal, natural manner.

Some thoughts may be positive, some negative, some may be related to your work, while others may surface without context. Keep your body steady regardless of the type of thoughts that arise.

Watch the thought, let it pass without chasing it, and silently utter the word "Next." The word "Next" acts as an anchor, allowing thoughts to reach their natural conclusion and dissolve.

Saying "Next" also raises your awareness of the gap between the thought that's receding and the next thought that's appearing. This interval may be as momentary as a thousandth of a second, but focus on that point regardless of the length of time.

In that interval there is no thought . . . everything has stopped and is frozen in that moment. In this gap, you begin to experience the silence, which is the background of thoughts.

When you're watching a passing train from the railway platform, you catch a glimpse of the opposite platform in the gaps between two cars. In the same way, you glimpse the silence presence in the gap between two thoughts.

You don't need to be worried if you miss the gap; instead, simply pay attention to the next thought and allow it to pass.

When you meditate but don't see any immediate results, you may become disappointed. The mind, in turn, may respond through an inability to concentrate. Focusing on thoughts of disappointment, though, will only drain your energy.

Remember: The goal is not a tangible result. The actual purpose is to become aware of the silent stillness by being in the gap between thoughts.

The key is to just watch these thoughts as if they were clouds passing by, momentarily shrouding the sunlight – clouds that are far away, that don't affect you. Observe these thoughts with a detached feeling, as if you are a witness watching them from afar.

You can practice this meditation whenever you have time at your disposal. It leads you into a receptive state, where you begin to receive the answers to your prayers.

Solution 16

Awaken Faith and Devotion

Certain problems shake your faith and devotion to the core. At such times, you need to recall, read, or listen to higher wisdom that helps strengthen your faith and devotion. For that, you may read books or listen to discourses or chant hymns. You may also count your blessings, which will make you receptive to grace. As you attune with vibrations of gratitude, faith and devotion in the midst of problems, nature gives you more of what you can be grateful for.

It is a fact of life - when faith is strong, the problem weakens; when your faith is weak, problems begin to dominate. Since we have to make one of these strong, let us strengthen faith.

Power of Faith

Faith is the highest vibration that humans can resonate with. Shallow faith is of no use. Faith needs to be solid and backed up with the wisdom of Truth. Faith springs from the heart, not the head. It is the essential fiber of life that cannot be rationalized or logically reasoned. Faith lies dormant until its amazing strength is called upon, empowering us to overcome the burden of problem situations. Faith makes it possible for us to persevere and endure anything and everything that comes our way.

Faith is the conviction that life is meant to attain the limitless potential that it is brimming with. Faith is the harbinger for a bright future. When your faith is unshaken, you are attuned with the Source of all creation. Your presence becomes like a magnet that attracts the highest and the best possibilities. You see abundance in life; everything is already available to be experienced. You then abound in the feeling of gratitude. You feel that nature which cares for all creatures is also taking care of all your needs, whether you are aware of your needs or not.

However, when you are faced with testing situations where things don't turn out as per your will, your faith quivers and doubts and despair sprout within you. You get into discord with nature's way of functioning. You feel negative emotions like sorrow and annoyance. You feel life is not leading you anywhere. At such times, even if it appears that faith is futile, yet, understand that you are preventing the best from flowing to you because of your lamenting. The first priority is to safeguard your happy natural state. In fact, these feelings are the indication from nature for you to realign with the flow of the Source. As you attune with the Source, your faith rebuilds and everything begins to fall into place.

Henceforth, when a calamity or a so-called problem befalls you, treat it as the real test of your faith. At such times, it is indeed a true test of faith to remain calm and composed, and trust what life holds in store for you. Have a deep assurance of abundance without worrying about scarcity of resources, ideas, time or connections. Such deep assurance is a manifestation of deep faith. With such assurance, you will see problems as opportunities to raise your faith.

There are thousands of people who have survived potentially disastrous situations where it would have been easy to give up.

Today, they point to faith and devotion in the Source as the relief that got them through to better times.

Power of Devotion

In our everyday life, we face many situations where emotions like anger, boredom, comparison, depression, ego, fear, guilt, hatred, ill will and jealousy overpower us. If someone gets angry with you and you too retaliate, then the situation deteriorates. At such time, it's better to stay calm. Further, if a person has said some hurtful words to you, then you may perhaps keep thinking about them for a long time and also think of getting even with him. Such a response gives rise to a tendency, which can harm you (not the other person) in the longer term.

When such tendencies overpower you, they don't let you see the other person as-is without any impressions of the past. As a result, you might tend to react at them instead of watching them afresh. If someone doesn't behave as per your will, you may perhaps become angry. When you become bored, you might engage yourself in entertainment, eating or chatting with your friends or go for shopping. Sometimes, it becomes nearly impossible to forgive any of your friends or relatives and you harbor resentment against them. You might even get into the crazy game of comparison and acquire those things, which are not at all your necessities. Thus, you spend time in worthless pursuits when you are overpowered by your tendencies and invite problems in turn.

The power of devotion plays an important role in such a scenario. You understand that whatever is happening in your life is by divine will. The situation has not come to push you down, but to raise you higher. It has come to make your body-mind free from vices and tendencies. It has come to teach you some important lessons of life after which new possibilities will unfold in your life. Trusting the Divine will, you give in to the flow of life, no matter what it brings you.

In love of the supreme power that runs the entire universe, you happily accept everything as a divine gift. The sweetness that is felt in devotion enables you to take the rough storms in the sea of life with a smile. The joy and rhythm rendered by devotion helps you tide over difficult circumstances and smoothly sail through the journey of life. You then are prepared to contemplate upon the situations and take necessary steps.

Despite the tendencies that drive you to behave in a programmed manner, you choose to shift your focus from the problematic situation and respond in a fresh way in favor of divine qualities like love, joy, peace, harmony, patience, courage, and communication.

In this way, you can choose to remain quiet instead of becoming angry. You can choose to feel compassionate for the other person instead of harboring hatred. You can choose to do some constructive work instead of indulging in sensual desires when the mind gets bored. Thus, devotion helps you escape from the quagmire of problematic situations, enabling you to lead a truly successful, peaceful, simple and straightforward life. You then look at the problematic situations as a hammer applied from outside to shape the pot of your life.

Whenever a problem arises, chant the name of God, your guru, or a higher power that you have faith on. You may bring their image in front of your eyes. By doing this, the tensions associated with the problem will diminish and the power of devotion will awaken within you. With the power of devotion, all the powers of the universe begin to work for you. The most difficult of tasks of the world get accomplished and the most difficult of issues get resolved.

Solution 17

Become a DS Master

When the sky is overcast, we see thick ominous clouds that remind us of thunderstorms. However, if we were to raise ourselves above this blanket of clouds, we would witness the ever-clear sky with bright sunshine. Similarly, when the clouds of trials and tribulations loom over us in everyday life, instead of worrying about life's problems, one should remember the immaculate sunshine and be confident that success is knocking at the door along with these challenges.

What happens when you watch the news on TV or read the newspaper? The negativity that is being dished out through media is served to your mind. Even if you hold these thoughts in your attention for a brief time, they are set up for manifesting in your life.

Most people believe that seeing is believing. They have to see things to believe them. However, the truth is that you get to see what you believe in. Your beliefs manifest in your experience. When you believe whatever the mind tells you, you get to see evidences of the same. Your world, as you perceive it, reflects the beliefs that are held in your mind.

All the negativity and limitations that we see around us are deluding scenes (DS) – be it clashes, floods, road accidents, traffic jams, failure, sickness, financial scarcity, confusion or anything else that appears negative. All these scenes are an illusory representation that causes impressions to form in your mind. They are all an illusion that results from negative interpretation – something which appears real, but in fact is not so.

Problem situations cause you to believe this illusion. You are overpowered by these deluding scenes. When you believe the deluding scenes to be real, they bring misery and block the free flow of positive things in your life.

In such testing situations, one may be forced to think, "Life is so difficult. How will my work be completed? Something very bad is happening to me. Violence is on the rise. The government will never be effective. People are careless and selfish. If only my wife would change herself…"

When one indulges in such thinking, they are unaware of the positive possibilities that are waiting to unfold; they are not conscious of the qualities of consciousness that lay dormant within them. Negative thoughts that are based on deluding scenes (DS) block new ideas from manifesting.

How can anything positive be created unless it's seen first at the level of thoughts? If we're busy in negative thinking, how can we even think of what we truly aspire to create? These DS-based thoughts keep us aloof from new flashes of inspiration that can help in overcoming testing situations.

At such times, you have to remind yourself that you are not the slave of illusion being created by limiting beliefs. You are the master of these deluding scenes (DS). You are a DS master. By merely remembering this, you can stop believing in it. Otherwise, the moment you start believing in it, you get swayed by the scenes and the problem comes into being out of nowhere. The problem may not exist, but no sooner do you believe it, than it begins to manifest its symptoms, magnifying the sense of the problem. Conversely, once you stop believing in it, the problem ceases to exist. When the disease retreats, healing begins. As soon as you remember that it is the illusory truth, the problem begins to fade away.

When you become a DS master, you learn to see the hidden truth behind the deluding scenes. When your focus is on the negative situations, you are unaware of the divine qualities that want to unfold through each of those situations. Happiness, love, peace, abundance, courage, success, wisdom, faith, smoothness, creativity, compassion, patience, communication, consistency, harmony are just a few of the many divine qualities.

How do you bring forth these diving qualities? By invoking them from the Source. Consciousness is the creative principle, the source of all possibilities. When engulfed by a deluding scene, choose to see the qualities of consciousness instead of focusing on the negative illusion. The shining sun, abundant harvest and ample food for all, cleanliness, compassion, love, courage, peace, patience, harmony, and creativity – all of which are qualities of consciousness – are welcomed. By choosing to focus on them, you invite those qualities into your life, not just for you but also for everyone around you. When you see these divine qualities, you are released from your overwhelmingly negative feelings.

Hereafter, if you face a challenging situation, ask yourself which divine quality is waiting to unfold in this situation. Invoke that quality. By doing this, you will change your vibrations to align with that quality and soon you will see yourself out of the situation. When you don't quiver in the face of the problem, the problem begins to quiver and fade away! This is the art of converting the

DS into an opportunity for expressing higher qualities. This will make you a DS master – someone who conquers deluding scenes by refusing to be cowed down.

Matchbox Value

Suppose you have gone to the market to buy a matchbox and the shopkeeper says the matchbox is worth five rupees. You tell the shopkeeper, "Five rupees is too much." You do not buy it because you know how much it is worth. When you refuse to pay five rupees for the matchbox, the shopkeeper tells you, "Ok. Take it for four rupees." But you will think, "Isn't four rupees also too much?" Till you do not know the true worth, you will continue to pay a high price. But when you come to know the real worth of the matchbox, you will negotiate and get the price down to its real worth.

In the same way, you need to evaluate the real worth of the situation when your mind blows the problem out of proportion. When the mind says that the problem appears like a huge monster and it's not possible to get out of it, understand that it is a deluding scene. Tell yourself, "I will not give undue worth to this situation. First let me evaluate the real worth of this situation." Evaluate the true worth of that situation and negotiate with the mind.

If you are getting agitated due to something, then ask yourself, "For how long should I be distressed with this problem?" Whatever answer you get, be troubled for only that much time and no more. If someone mouthed abuses at you or someone did not complete the task that you had asked him to, then ask yourself, "For how long should I be upset with this? How much value should I give to this matter?" You will get the answer from within based on your understanding. Suppose you get the answer, "I should be upset with this matter for at least ten minutes." You will allow the mind to be upset for ten minutes, not a minute more.

Value a thing only to the extent that is due to it. Being able to decide how much value you should give to any thing is the hallmark of maturity. If you can choose the time for which you will be upset, then you will feel that being upset for even ten minutes is too much. After that you will reduce that time as well. When you do this consciously, you will see that you will not be as disappointed as you used to earlier. When you have a choice of being upset, you will find it unnecessary to be upset even for a minute. This will happen automatically after attaining emotional maturity.

Solution 18

Surrender

Imagine a scene where a child is playing with toys in a room. Some of his toys are broken. Others are scattered all around. His clothes, toys, his school bag, books, paintbrush, pens are all scattered. Nothing is in order. But when the child falls asleep, his mother comes and neatly arranges everything. How did the child help in this situation? The child helped by being silent and sleeping.

The child demonstrates a key skill, which is the most potent way of going through life's trials cheerfully. And that is the state of being surrendered to the flow of life. This is something that the logical and rational mind cannot reason. The mind will be quick to interject – how can we surrender the situation passively and expect solutions to our problems?

Surrender has been a grossly misunderstood secret, due to which the beauty of what happens with true surrender is lost to the reasoning intellect. Surrender is seen as the need to submit to something or someone, due to which it is seen as a form of weakness. It is seen as a sign of defeat.

Much against this notion, surrender is the gateway to immense power. It opens you to the highest possibilities that can manifest in your life. True surrender is an absolute state. When the limited intellect surrenders the entire situation including its concerns to the

Source of life, it is like handing over a matchstick to an elephant. The elephant can handle it immensely and effortlessly!

Due to ignorance, human beings feel that they are individually functioning for themselves and that they have an existence independent of the whole. But it is only through surrender that we realize that we all are merely instrumental for the purpose of the Source of life.

Consciousness is the Source of life, also known in other terms as God or Higher Self. The Source functions through all of us. To put things in the right perspective, when we think, breathe, and are self-aware, the Source of life is living *through* us. We are no different from the Source.

When we consider whatever is inside our skin to be "I" and everything that is outside our skin to be "other," we do not recognize our true nature. We believe that we are leading life. The truth is that consciousness enlivens this story called "my life".

When we consider ourselves separate from the Source of life, we limit ourselves to birth and death. When we become one with life in the state of surrender, we allow life to blossom and express through us. Allow life to happen, rather than pre-determining how life should be. Allow solutions to arise intuitively from the wellspring of consciousness instead of dwelling in the logical confines of problems.

You may ask, "Does this mean that we should just go with the flow? Then we become like leaves in the wind, swirling here and there?" Contrary to this, when you realize the real magnitude of the Source, you attain a state of true freedom. By surrendering to the Source, you reach a standpoint where you see the drama of life unfolding and direct life creatively.

In today's increasingly fast-paced world, man experiences a lot of stress, misery, anxiety, demands and struggles. By surrendering to the Source, you can let go of all struggle and just allow life to unfold. The most powerful creative potential begins to express itself through you. The best solutions to problems begin to spontaneously unravel themselves.

Just like the child in the earlier example, you too can emulate him by being quiet and surrendering to Mother Nature. Take a look at the problems in your life. There may be problems related to relationships, health, wealth, neighborhood or the country. All the problems are scattered, just like the child's toys. When you know the highest way of solving these problems, you will give an opportunity for the Source to function.

You will think, "Now, I will keep quiet. It would have been good if I were allowed to do something. But, as work is done best when I am quiet, I will now remain quiet. I will allow the Source to work on the problem. Let the Source express itself in every aspect of my life – be it the emotional aspect, mental, physical, financial, social, and spiritual."

In this way, you repose your unflinching faith in the Source (God) and allow it to function through you. Since you have handed the responsibility over to the "best of hands", you need not worry any more. You are now open to any outcome that unfolds before you, regardless of your preferences.

Many people remark how they have benefitted from this sutra of surrender. They completely surrendered their problems with the firm conviction that the supreme consciousness can never falter. They remain mentally relaxed, while they may continue to work physically. In their relaxed state of inner calmness everything starts falling in place.

5

The Ultimate Remedy to Dissolve Your Problems

We have looked at eighteen solutions that can help in bringing solutions to problems. We will now look at the ultimate solution, which does not solve problems, but dissolves them! You may wonder how this can be achieved. This is possible when we abide in the Source within us.

To understand what the Source is, let's first consider who we truly are. Are you the physical body? Your legs, your hands, your face, your trunk, is that you? Careful observation will show that we are not our bodies, since we can observe our bodies. Whatever is being observed is not the observer.

Are you your mind then? The constant stream of thoughts that arises within you… is that you? Again, if you observe closely, it is not difficult to see that even your thoughts can be observed as separate things. You can take some time out to observe your thoughts as they arise and subside. As you practice this, you discover that you are not your thoughts. You are not just the thinking machine called "mind". Rather the thinking machine is an instrument that you use. You are the knower of your thoughts, the knower of your mind. This knowing continues to exist even in the gap between thoughts.

Other names for this knowing that is happening constantly is awareness or consciousness. Consciousness is the essence of life. It is the Source of life. Everything arises from this Source. It is who-you-truly-are, beyond your body and mind. Consciousness can be experienced as the feeling of *beingness*, of being awake to whatever is happening. This song of *beingness* is being played constantly; you are that song. When consciousness awakens to itself, when you (consciousness) are aware of your true nature, you experience pure joy, unconditional and boundless, independent of the world, untouched by situations.

Our *beingness* is the Source of creation; it is the wellspring of inspiration. When we do not tap into this, our thoughts tend to be limited by what we see in the world. We are shut off to novelty. We look at situations through the lens of our beliefs and build resistance. Our thinking mind tends to give situations undue importance by resisting it. Resistance causes the undesired situation to persist. This is the main cause of problems. Seeing the situation as a problem is the only real problem.

The constant chatter of the mind is the real problem by itself. Thoughts impress upon our awareness and cause awareness to be consumed by situations. When we dismiss these very thoughts, we find to our surprise that there is no problem!

You can dismiss your thoughts in an effortless manner with the understanding that thoughts by themselves have no power to hurt you. Thoughts contain content. As long as we perceive thoughts as just thoughts, there is no problem. The problem starts when we focus on the content of our thoughts. You may dismiss one thought as insignificant, yet you hold onto another as if it had a life of its own. It doesn't. One thought can be dismissed just as easily as another. Whenever you take a thought seriously, regardless of the content, you set yourself up to experience the effects of that thought and to feel the emotions tied to it.

When we begin to realize how we emotionally trouble ourselves with our own thinking, we will begin to set ourselves free. We then start seeing all thoughts just as thoughts. If we are the source of our own thoughts, then these thoughts themselves have no life of their own and cannot harm us. All problems are thought created. We manufacture and blow problems out of proportion. If we can step outside the boundaries of our own thinking and abide in the awareness of our pure Being, we can tap into the source of intuition.

Problems that occur at a given level of awareness can never be resolved at the same level of awareness. With pure witnessing from a higher awareness, the problem no longer remains a problem. You begin to witness the beliefs and notions that are distorting your view, causing you to see it as a problem.

While you dismiss your thoughts, you get an opportunity to dip into the inner stillness of consciousness. By abiding in the Source, you learn the true way of addressing problems, instead of escaping them. By being in the Source, you allow the problematic situation to settle in the space of acceptance. You no longer resist it. You don't get into a discord. You remain in joyous harmony with the flow of whatever is happening. You remain aware of whatever is, without attaching any special meaning to it.

When you lend your detached presence through this way of witnessing, the solution emerges from the so-called "problem" situation itself. Thus, by being in the Source you don't solve problems, rather you dissolve them. Your thoughts and actions are then imbued with freshness, delight, creativity and inspiration. You remain away from confusion, anxiety, overstimulation, and being enmeshed in the quagmire of your own thinking. You always remain happy and peaceful.

If the solution demands action, you will then witness all the necessary actions happening through you or whoever else participates in the scene. You have to experience how solutions unfold from problem situations when you abide in the witnessing presence. This will build conviction in your nature as pure *beingness*.

As you start living in your happy natural state of *beingness*, you will not be concerned with what happens in your life. Instead, you will be more concerned about how you relate to it.

Let's understand this with an example.

A person received a bunch of mails in the morning and started opening them one by one. The first mail was the electricity bill. The inflated amount on the electricity bill infuriated him and he scolded his family members, "You unnecessarily waste electricity. You forget to switch off the water heater. You keep the fans running even when you are not in the rooms. You keep watching cricket matches, movies and TV serials till late night. Now who will pay this electricity bill?"

Same was the case with the grocer's bill. He rebuked them, "You keep drinking tea any time without any measure. There is no limit to the food you waste. Do you know the prices of foodstuff and vegetables? You don't know how much I have to work hard to make both ends meet."

There was also a letter from his son's school principal. His fees were not paid. He admonished his son, "There is so much expenditure. Now where will I get the money to pay your fees? You simply play throughout the day. When will you take your studies seriously?"

All the members were scared of him. At the end, he opened the last envelope to find a note announcing that he had won a lottery worth 10 million. He got the solution to all his problems in this envelope. At this, he jumped with joy and in his delight, called his entire family together and rejoiced.

Just imagine the envelope was already with him when he was going through all the other mail. The solution to his problems was there with him even while he was in distress, fretting and fuming at his family members. Had he known about this envelope, would he have troubled himself as well as his family members so much?

As soon as he came to know about his winning the lottery, all his problems dissolved at once. His attitude towards his family also changed. Love, joy, contentment and harmony had taken the place of distress, anger, blame and disharmony. Now, he asked his son to take more money for his books, his wife to buy more milk for his son. His approach completely changed after he got to know about the lottery.

Most people lead a similar life. Despite having boundless joy within, they live in perpetual tension and see problems everywhere in their vicinity. They need to understand that they don't have to solve these problems, rather they need to dissolve them. As you become clear about this, the secret of life would be as apparent to you as the daylight. Here is another example to understand this.

In the kingdom of Mithila ruled the wise King Janaka. One night, the king had a vivid dream. He was fighting a war and his army was vanquished; he fled from the battle field. Running through the jungle for hours, he was exhausted and hungry. He found some food and was about to eat it when a wild boar charged at him, screaming and gnawing at him.

King Janaka cried in pain. He could not take it any more... and he woke up! To his surprise, he found himself resting in comfort in his royal bed in the palace.

For the king, everything had become questionable. "Was that a dream, or is this a dream?" He wondered, "Is it possible that I am actually starving in the jungle after fleeing from battle, and dreaming that I am enjoying the luxuries of this palace? What is the reality?"

He consulted his advisors, the learned pundits of his kingdom, but none could provide a satisfactory answer. Finally, Sage Ashtavakra visited the royal palace when he found that many pundits were being put to trial.

He revealed the truth of existence, "O Rajarishi! Few are those fortunate ones who live in luxuries and yet ponder the profound truth of life. You are a king and also a Rishi (one who grasps the secret of life). This question that has gripped you is auspicious. Many would laugh this away, but few will be able to discern the depth of this question."

The sage then continued, "Neither this, nor that is real. Both are dreams, both are changing. That which you truly are is permanent, all-pervading, alive and conscious. It is the source of everything. Everything else is temporary, limited and unreal. Experiencing this reality dispels all doubts and gives lasting peace and bliss. Dwelling in doubts and trying to reason only raises more doubts and causes restlessness."

Do the first thing first. First realize who you truly are. Then you will realize that none of the problems are yours. The problems are with your body-mind, not with you. You are separate from your body-mind. Just as waves arise and subside in the ocean, by abiding in your true nature – the Source – you witness problems arising and dissolving on their own. Problem solving will then become a matter of joy, Self-expression and opportunity for you. When a problem doesn't remain a problem anymore, then the problem doesn't even need to be solved.

Hereafter, don't get bogged down by problems. Learn the art of dissolving problems which will make you stronger. Thereafter, solving problems will not become a work for you, rather it will become an expression of joy for you.

■ ■ ■

You can send your opinion or feedback on this book to:

Tejgyan Foundation Pimpri Colony, P. O. Box 25
Pimpri, Pune – 411017 (Maharashtra), INDIA
Email: mail@tejgyan.com

Write for Us

We welcome writers, translators and editors to join our team. If you would like to volunteer, please email us at: englishbooks@tejgyan.org or call : +91 90110 10963 or +91 90110 13207

About Sirshree

Sirshree's spiritual quest which began during his childhood, led him on a journey through various schools of thought and meditation practices. His overpowering desire to attain the truth made him relinquish his teaching job. After a long period of contemplation, his spiritual quest culminated in the attainment of the ultimate truth. Sirshree says, **"All paths that lead to the truth begin differently, but end in the same way—with understanding. Understanding is the whole thing. Listening to this understanding is enough to attain the truth."**

Sirshree is the author of several spiritual books. His books have been translated in more than10 languages and published by leading publishers such as Penguin and Hay House.

He is the founder of Tej Gyan Foundation, a not-for-profit organization committed to raising mass consciousness by spreading "Happy Thoughts" with branches in the United States, India, Europe and Asia-Pacific. Sirshree's retreats have transformed the lives of thousands and his teachings have inspired various social initiatives for raising global consciousness.

His works include more than 100 books and 3000 discourses. Various luminaries such as His Holiness the Dalai Lama, publishers Reid Tracy and Tami Simon and yoga master Dr. B. K. S Iyengar have released Sirshree's books and lauded his work. His book *The Warrior's Mirror*, published by Penguin, was featured in the Limca Book of Records for being released on the same day in 10 languages.

Tejgyan... The Road Ahead

What is Tejgyan?

Tejgyan is the existential wisdom of the ultimate truth, which is beyond duality. In today's world, there are people who feel disharmony and are desperately trying to achieve balance in an unpredictable life. Tejgyan helps them in harmonizing with their true nature, the Self, thereby restoring balance in all aspects of their life.

And then there are those who are successful but feel a sense of emptiness or void within. Tejgyan provides them fulfillment and helps them to embark on a journey towards self-realization. There are others who feel lost and are seeking the meaning of life. Tejgyan helps them to realize the true purpose of human life.

All this is possible with Tejgyan due to a very simple reason. The experience of the ultimate truth is always available. The direct experience of this truth is possible provided the right method is known. Tejgyan is that method, that understanding. At Tej Gyan Foundation, Sirshree imparts this understanding through a System for Wisdom – a series of retreats that guides participants step by step

Magic of Awakening Retreat

Magic of Awakening is the flagship self-realization retreat offered by Tej Gyan Foundation The retreat is conducted in two languages – Hindi and English. The teachings of the retreat are non-denominational (secular).

This residential retreat is held for 3-5 days at the foundation's MaNaN Ashram amidst the glory of mountains and the pristine nature. This ashram is located at the outskirts of the city of Pune in India, and is well connected by air, road and rail. The retreat is also held at other centres of Tej Gyan Foundation across the world.

Participate in the *Magic of Awakening* retreat to attain ageless wisdom through a unique simple 'System for Wisdom' so that you can:

1. Live from pure and still presence allowing the natural qualities of consciousness, viz. peace, love, joy, compassion, abundance and creativity to manifest.

2. Acquire simple tools to use in everyday life which help quieten the chattering mind, revealing your true nature.

3. Get practical techniques to access pure presence at will and connect to the source of all answers (the inner guru).

4. Discover missing links in practices of meditation *(dhyana)*, action *(karma)*, wisdom *(gyana)* and devotion *(bhakti)*.

5. Understand the nature of your body-mind mechanism to attain freedom from tendencies and patterns.

6. Learn practical methods to shift from mind-centred living to consciousness-centred living.

For retreats contact +919921008060 or email: mail@tejgyan.com

A Mini retreat is also conducted, especially for teens (14-17 years) during summer and winter vacations

MaNaN Ashram

Survey No. 43, Sanas Nagar, Nandoshi gaon, Kirkatwadi Phata, Sinhagad Road, Dist. Pune 411024, Maharashtra, India.

About Tej Gyan Foundation

Tej Gyan Foundation (TGF) was established with the mission of creating a highly evolved society through all-round self development of every individual that transforms all the facets of his/her life. It is a non-profit organization founded on the teachings of Sirshree. The foundation has received the ISO certification (ISO 9001:2015) for its system of imparting wisdom. It has centres all across India as well as in other countries. The motto of Tej Gyan Foundation is 'Happy Thoughts'.

TGF is creating a highly evolved society through:

- Tejgyan Programs (Retreats, Courses, Television and Radio Programs, Podcasts)

- Tejgyan Products (Books, Tapes, Audio/Video CDs)

- Tejgyan Projects (Value Education, Women Empowerment, Peace Initiatives)

TGF undertakes projects to elevate the level of consciousness among students, youth, women, senior citizens, teachers, doctors, leaders, organizations, police force, prisoners, etc.

Now you can register online for the following retreats

Maha Aasmani Niwasi Shivir
(5 Days Residential Retreat in Hindi)

Magic of Awakening Retreat
(3 Days Residential Retreat In English)

Mini Maha Aasmani Shivir
3 Days (Residential) Retreat for Teens

🔍 www.tejgyan.org

Books can be delivered at your doorstep by registered post or courier. You can request for the same through postal money order or pay by VPP. Please send the money order to either of the following two addresses:

WOW Publishings Pvt. Ltd.

1. Registered Office: E-4, Vaibhav Nagar, Near Tapovan Mandir, Pimpri, Pune 411017.

2. Post Box No. 36, Pimpri Colony Post Office, Pimpri, , Pune 411017

Phone No. : 9011013210 / 9623457873

You can also order your copy at the online store:

www.gethappythoughts.org

*Free Shipping plus 10% Discount on purchases above Rs. 300/-.

For further details contact:

Tejgyan Global Foundation

Registered Office:
Happy Thoughts Building, Vikrant Complex, Near
Tapovan Mandir, Pimpri, Pune 411017, Maharashtra, India.
Contact No: 020-27411240, 27412576
Email: mail@tejgyan.com

MaNaN Ashram:
Survey No. 43, Sanas Nagar, Nandoshi gaon, Kirkatwadi Phata,
Sinhagad Road, Tal. Haveli, Dist. Pune 411024, Maharashtra, India.
Contact No: 992100 8060.

Hyderabad: 9885558100, **Bangalore:** 9880412588,

Delhi: 9891059875, **Nashik:** 9326967980, **Mumbai:** 9373440985

For accessing our unique 'System for Wisdom' from self-help to self-realization, please follow us on:

	Website	www.tejgyan.org
You Tube	Video Channel	www.youtube.com/tejgyan For Q&A videos: http://goo.gl/YA81DQ
facebook	Social networking	www.facebook.com/tejgyan
twitter	Social networking	www.twitter.com/sirshree
	Internet Radio	http://www.tejgyan.org internetradio.aspx

Online Shopping
www.gethappythoughts.org

Pray for World Peace along with thousands of others at 09:09 a.m. and p.m. every day

www.ingramcontent.com/pod-product-compliance
Lightning Source LLC
LaVergne TN
LVHW040157080526
838202LV00042B/3203